HBJ TREASURY OF LITERATURE

GRAND OPENING

SENIOR AUTHORS
ROGER C. FARR
DOROTHY S. STRICKLAND

AUTHORS
RICHARD F. ABRAHAMSON
ELLEN BOOTH CHURCH
BARBARA BOWEN COULTER
MARGARET A. GALLEGO
JUDITH L. IRVIN
KAREN KUTIPER
JUNKO YOKOTA LEWIS
DONNA M. OGLE
TIMOTHY SHANAHAN
PATRICIA SMITH

SENIOR CONSULTANTS
BERNICE E. CULLINAN
W. DORSEY HAMMOND
ASA G. HILLIARD III

CONSULTANTS
ALONZO A. CRIM
ROLANDO R. HINOJOSA-SMITH
LEE BENNETT HOPKINS
ROBERT J. STERNBERG

 HARCOURT BRACE JOVANOVICH, INC.
Orlando Austin San Diego Chicago Dallas New York

Printed in the United States of America

ISBN 0-15-301475-X

1 2 3 4 5 6 7 8 9 10   048   96   95   94   93   92

Acknowledgments
For permission to reprint copyrighted material, grateful acknowledgment is made to the following sources:
Carolrhoda Books, Inc., Minneapolis, MN: How the Guinea Fowl Got Her Spots by Barbara Knutson. Copyright 1990 by Barbara Knutson.
Dutton Children's Books, a division of Penguin Books USA Inc.: Our Home Is the Sea by Riki Levinson, illustrated by Dennis Luzak. Text copyright © 1988 by Riki Friedberg Levinson; illustrations copyright © 1988 by Dennis Luzak.
GRM Associates, Inc., Agents for Children's Book Press: Baby Rattlesnake by Lynn Moroney, illustrated by Veg Reisberg. Text copyright © 1989 by Lynn Moroney; illustrations copyright © 1989 by Veg Reisberg.
Holiday House: The Great Trash Bash by Loreen Leedy. Copyright © 1991 by Loreen Leedy.
Scholastic Inc.: Effie by Beverley Allinson, illustrated by Barbara Reid. Text copyright © 1990 by Beverley Allinson; illustrations copyright © 1990 by Barbara Reid. *The Hole in the Dike*, retold by Norma Green. Text copyright © 1974 by Norma B. Green.

Photograph Credits
Key: (t) top, (b) bottom, (l) left, (c) center, (r) right.
HBJ Photo 50, 100, 130.

Illustration Credits
Key: (t) top, (b) bottom, (l) left, (c) center, (r) right.

Table of Contents Art
Gerald McDermott, 4 (bl); Sue Williams, 4 (tl), 4–5 (c) (r).

Unit Opening Patterns
Dan Thoner

Selection Art
Barbara Knutson, 6–25; Veg Reisberg, 26–47; Dennis Luzak, 52–73, Roseanne Litzinger, 74–99; Barbara Reid, 102–129; Loreen Leedy, 132–159.

Dear Reader,

Welcome to the grand opening of a reading adventure! Come with us as we explore different places and cultures.

Our world is made up of so many different things. There is always something new to learn. In this book you will read about places near and far and the people and animals that live there. You will visit Africa, Holland, and many more places. You will follow a boy through the streets of Hong Kong. You will hear a conversation between an elephant and an ant! You will even help clean up a town!

Look closely at the beautiful pictures in Grand Opening. You'll enjoy reading the stories over and over again. Join us on an exciting adventure.

Sincerely,
The Authors

C O N T E N T S

UNIT ONE/UNUSUAL ZOO

How the Guinea Fowl Got Her Spots / 6
retold and illustrated by Barbara Knutson
Pourquoi Tale

Baby Rattlesnake / 26
told by Te Ata
Folktale

Words About the Storyteller: Te Ata / 48

UNIT TWO/WORLD CORNERS

Our Home Is the Sea / 50
written by Riki Levinson
Realistic Fiction

The Hole in the Dike / 74
retold by Norma Green
illustrated by Roseanne Litzinger
Folktale

UNIT THREE/SIDE BY SIDE

Effie / 100
written by Beverley Allinson
Fantasy

The Great Trash Bash / 130
written and illustrated by Loreen Leedy
Nonfiction

Glossary / 161

How the Guinea Fowl Got Her Spots

A SWAHILI TALE OF FRIENDSHIP RETOLD AND ILLUSTRATED BY

BARBARA KNUTSON

A long time ago,
when everything had just been made,
Nganga the Guinea Fowl had
glossy black feathers all over.
She had no white speckles
as she does today—
not a single spot.

uinea Fowl was a little bird,
but she had a big friend.
And that was Cow.

They liked to go to the great
green hills where Cow
could eat grass and
Nganga could scratch for seeds
and crunch grasshoppers.
                    And they would both
                    keep an eye out for Lion.

8

One day, Guinea Fowl was crossing the river to meet Cow on the most delicious hill they knew. The grass was so juicy and thick that, even from the river, Nganga could hear Cow hungrily tearing up one mouthful after another.

9

But . . .

what was that
Nganga saw
slinking toward Cow?

Was it . . . ?
Yes, it was LION!

Now you might think a guinea fowl is no match for a lion, but Nganga didn't think that. In fact, she didn't think at all. She scratched and scrambled up the bank as fast as she could and whirred right between Cow and Lion, kicking and flapping in the dust.

"RAAUGH!" shouted Lion.
"My eyes! This sand! What was that?"

When the clouds of dust thinned
there was no sign of anyone—
certainly not any dinner for Lion.
He went home in a terrible temper,
growling like his empty belly.

The next day, Guinea Fowl was at the grassy patch first. You can be sure she had her eyes wide open for Lion.

Soon she saw Cow cautiously crossing the river to join her— shlip, clop, shlop. But something yellow was twitching in the reeds. Wasn't that Lion's tail?

U p whirred Nganga, half tumbling,
half flying with her stubby wings.
Lion looked up, startled,
from his hiding place.
Frrr . . . a little black whirlwind
    was racing across the grass
        toward the river.
            "Whe-klo-klo-klo!"
            it called out to Cow.

"Guinea Fowl! That's where the duststorm came from yesterday," growled Lion between his sharp teeth. But the next moment, the whirlwind hit the river.

"RAAUghmf!" Lion exploded with a roar that ended underwater.

"**I**'ll teach that bird to chase away my dinner!" he spluttered. But by the time his roar

Glurmf!

Rgmf!

RAAglf!

was working

RAAUGH!

properly again,

Cow and Guinea Fowl
were safely over the next
hill at Cow's house.

Nganga," mooed Cow gratefully, "twice you have helped me escape from Lion. Now I will help you do the same."

Turning around, she dipped her tasseled tail into a calabash of milk. Then she shook the tasselful of milk over Guinea Fowl's sleek black feathers—flick, flock, flick—spattering her with creamy white milk.

Guinea Fowl craned her head
and admired the delicate speckles
covering her back.

She spread her wings,

and Cow sprinkled them with milk too—
flick, flock, flick.
    "Whe-klo-klo!
That's beautiful, Cow!"
chuckled Nganga.
"Thank you, my friend!"
And she set off for home.

Whom should she meet
where the path crossed the river
but Lion, still shaking
the water out of his ears
and angrier than ever.
"Ho, Speckled Bird!"
snorted Lion.
"Have you seen Guinea Fowl
on your path?"

"Oh yes," clucked Nganga, hiding a smile.
"I believe she went that way."
She pointed with her spotted wing
to the hills far down the river.
"If you go quickly and don't stop
to rest, you may catch up with her
in a few days."

L

ion leaped up at once,
not bothering to thank the strange bird.

A minute later, he thought
about taking her along for a
traveling snack, but when he looked
back at the riverbank, he could see no trace of her.

These lovely spots are just the thing for hiding in the shadows and grass!" laughed Nganga, who was, in fact, right where Lion had left her.

And she turned back
to Cow's house
to thank her friend
again.

Baby Rattlesnake

TOLD BY TE ATA

ADAPTED BY LYNN MORONEY

ILLUSTRATED BY VEG REISBERG

O ut in the place where the rattlesnakes lived, there was a little baby rattlesnake who cried all the time because he did not have a rattle.

He said to his mother and father, "I don't know why I don't have a rattle. I'm made just like my brother and sister. How can I be a rattlesnake if I don't have a rattle?"

Mother and Father Rattlesnake said, "You are too young to have a rattle. When you get to be as old as your brother and sister, you will have a rattle, too."

But Baby Rattlesnake did not want to wait. So he just cried and cried. He shook his tail and when he couldn't hear a rattle sound, he cried even louder.

Mother and Father said, "Shhh! Shhh! Shhhhh!"

Brother and Sister said, "Shhh! Shhh! Shhhhh!"

But Baby Rattlesnake wouldn't stop crying. He kept the Rattlesnake People awake all night.

The next morning, the Rattlesnake People called a big council. They talked and they talked just like people do, but they couldn't decide how to make that little baby rattlesnake happy. He didn't want anything else but a rattle.

At last one of the elders said, "Go ahead, give him a rattle. He's too young and he'll get into trouble. But let him learn a lesson. I just want to get some sleep."

So they gave Baby Rattlesnake a rattle.

Baby Rattlesnake loved his rattle. He shook his tail and for the first time he heard, "Ch-Ch-Ch! Ch-Ch-Ch!" He was so excited!

He sang a rattle song, "Ch-Ch-Ch! Ch-Ch-Ch!"

He danced a rattle dance, "Ch-Ch-Ch! Ch-Ch-Ch!"

Soon Baby Rattlesnake learned
to play tricks with his rattle.
He hid in the rocks and when
the small animals came by,
he darted out rattling,
"Ch-Ch-Ch!" "Ch-Ch-Ch!"

He made Jack Rabbit jump.
He made Old Man Turtle jump.
He made Prairie Dog jump.

Each time Baby Rattlesnake
laughed and laughed. He
thought it was fun to scare the
animal people.

ha ha

other and Father warned Baby Rattlesnake, "You must not use your rattle in such a way."

Big Brother and Big Sister said, "You are not being careful with your rattle."

The Rattlesnake People told Baby Rattlesnake to stop acting so foolish with his rattle.

Baby Rattlesnake did not listen.

One day, Baby Rattlesnake said to his mother and father, "How will I know a chief's daughter when I see her?"

"Well, she's usually very beautiful and walks with her head held high," said Father.

"And she's very neat in her dress," added Mother.

"Why do you want to know?" asked Father.

"Because I want to scare her!" said Baby Rattlesnake. And he started right off down the path before his mother and father could warn him never to do a thing like that.

The little fellow reached the place where the Indians traveled. He curled himself up on a log and he started rattling. "Chh-Chh-Chh!" He was having a wonderful time.

All of a sudden he saw a beautiful maiden coming toward him from a long way off. She walked with her head held high, and she was very neat in her dress.

"Ah," thought Baby Rattlesnake. "She must be the chief's daughter."

Baby Rattlesnake hid in the rocks. He was excited. This was going to be his best trick.

He waited and waited. The chief's daughter came closer and closer. When she was in just the right spot, he darted out of the rocks.

"Ch-Ch-Ch-Ch-Ch!"

Ho!" cried the chief's daughter. She whirled around, stepping on Baby Rattlesnake's rattle and crushing it to pieces.

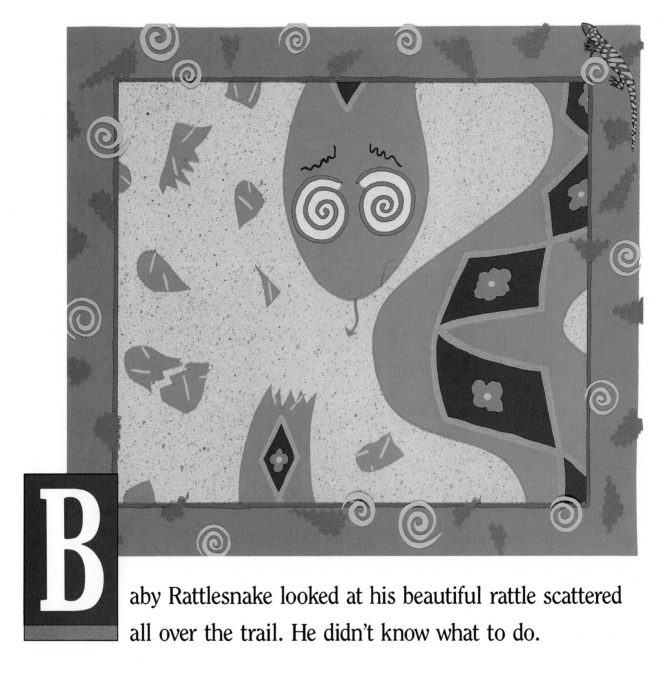

Baby Rattlesnake looked at his beautiful rattle scattered all over the trail. He didn't know what to do.

He took off for home as fast as he could.

ith great sobs, he told Mother and Father what had happened. They wiped his tears and gave him big rattlesnake hugs.

For the rest of that day, Baby Rattlesnake stayed safe and snug, close by his rattlesnake family.

47

Words About the Storyteller: Te Ata

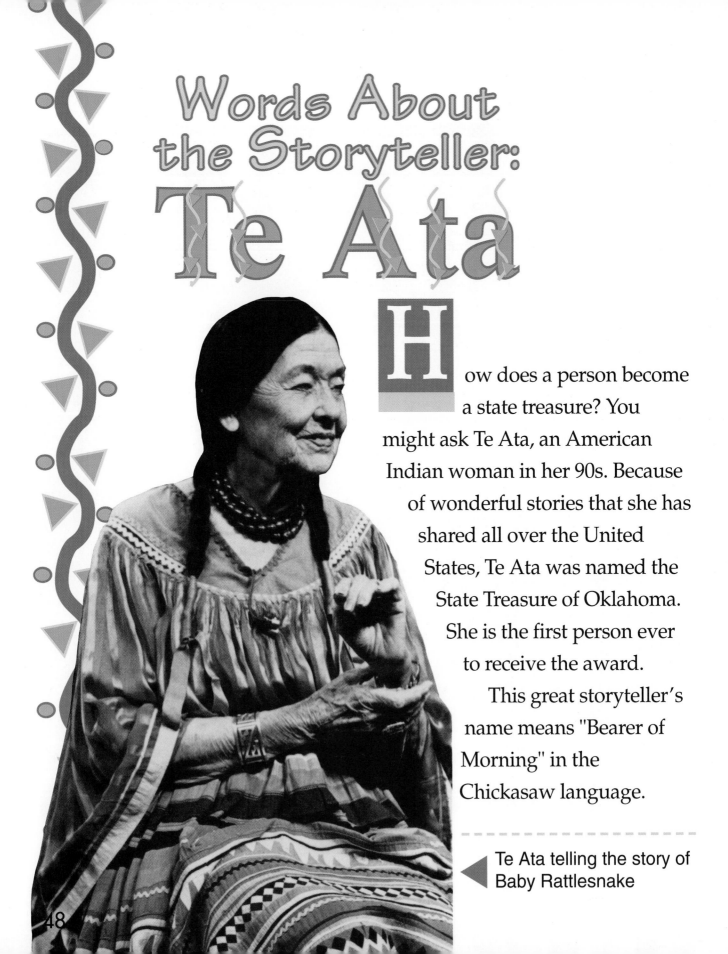

How does a person become a state treasure? You might ask Te Ata, an American Indian woman in her 90s. Because of wonderful stories that she has shared all over the United States, Te Ata was named the State Treasure of Oklahoma. She is the first person ever to receive the award.

This great storyteller's name means "Bearer of Morning" in the Chickasaw language.

◀ Te Ata telling the story of Baby Rattlesnake

48

Te Ata's parents helped her become a great storyteller. Her mother taught her the beauty of the ways of the Indians. Her father passed on to her the old Indian tales. On cold nights, Te Ata and the other children would gather around a fire. They begged to hear the story of Grandfather Turtle or Baby Rattlesnake.

When Te Ata grew up she began to tell her American Indian tales. She started with the stories told by her father and mother. She added songs, legends, and history. She used many different voices to tell her stories. She went around the country visiting Indian schools and celebrations. She told about the beginnings of the Indians and about their ways. She told stories like "Baby Rattlesnake" that teach lessons. More important, she listened to people wherever she went.

People loved Te Ata and her stories so much that she was invited to tell them to many famous people. Eleanor Roosevelt, the wife of President Franklin D. Roosevelt even named a lake in New York State after Te Ata.

Now Te Ata has returned to live in Oklahoma, the home of the Chickasaw Nation. She feels that her storytelling helps people understand American Indians. She hopes that it also helps American Indians understand themselves better.

OUR HOME IS THE SEA

Riki Levinson

Paintings by Dennis Luzak

Our home is the sea, grandfather said to my father, and father said to me.

I am the eldest son, just like my father. When he was a boy, he did not go to school. I wish I didn't have to. I could be with my father all the time.

Soon he will come for me, for today is my last day of school.

I stuff my report card into a pocket. I do not want my mother to see it. She will say that I will be a schoolteacher someday. That is not what I want to be.

I stand on the hill near my school. I can see the sea. My sea.

Down, down the hill I run, to take the tram home.

I get on the tram quickly,
run up the stairs, and sit down to
watch.

The tram moves slowly. I
cannot wait.

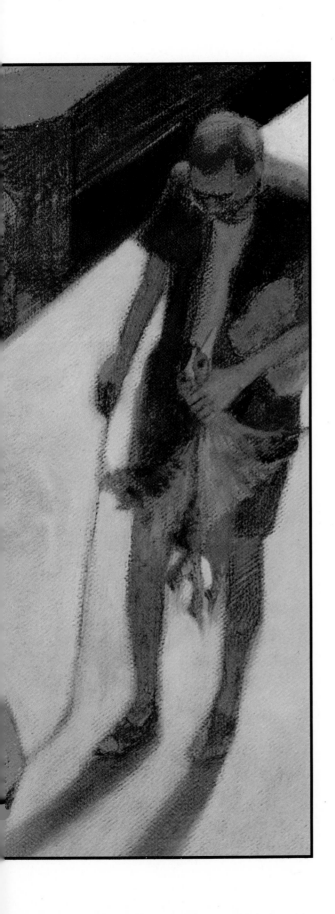

We ride through market streets. People crowd around the carts.

A mother with a baby strapped on her back bends up and down, up and down. The baby sleeps.

A man walks through the street carrying two birds. They make loud noises. I do not think they like to be carried by their necks.

At the end of the street, the tram stops. The light is red.

A school bus crosses to the other side of the road.

Little children hop off the bus. Amahs are waiting to take them home.

I cannot wait for the light to turn green.

The tram turns slowly onto a wide street, past tall houses with windows full of plants and drying clothes. I would not want to live in a tall house.

I watch for the park.

When the tram stops, I hurry down the stairs and get off.

I run to the park.

I see an old man standing straight and still under a gingko tree. Slowly he lifts his arms and sweeps them around, and stands still again. He looks like a bird.

As quietly as I can, I walk past the old man.

I see the birdmen come and hang their cages on a low berry tree. The men sit down to talk. I think the birds talk to each other too.

I see the peacocks. One comes near and stares at me. I stare back. The peacock lifts its head and spreads its feathers wide. I spread my arms. I wish I had feathers like the peacock.

At the end of the park, I run up the long steps and cross over the harbor road. I can see our house on the water. I wave. Middle brother and little brother wave back as I run down the steps to the wharf.

I put my schoolbag down, take off my shoes, and wait for mother to come. She poles our sampan to the water's edge. I step down into our little boat to go home.

When we get there, I put my schoolbag away. I will not need it for a long time.

Middle brother and little brother and I sit down on the floor. Mother fills our bowls with congee and pours the tea.

The night mist falls gently down as we eat.

I go to bed early. I cannot wait for tomorrow. My father will come, back from the sea.

Early in the morning, I hear my mother and father talking. I get out of bed quickly and go to him. He puts his hand on my shoulder. I am glad he is near me.

After we eat, we climb down into our sampan and ride out, past the jetty, to grandfather's big boat.

Father and I climb up the ladder.

Mother calls and tells him I will be a schoolteacher someday.

I look at my father. He looks at me. We do not say a word.

I will be a fisherman, like my father and grandfather. Our home is the sea.

THE HOLE IN THE DIKE

Retold by Norma Green
Illustrated by Rosanne Litzinger

A long time ago, a boy named Peter lived in Holland. He lived with his mother and father in a cottage next to a tulip field.

Peter loved to look at the old windmills turning slowly.

He loved to look at the sea.

In Holland, the land is very low, and the sea is very high. The land is kept safe and dry by high, strong walls called dikes.

One day Peter went to visit a friend who lived by the seaside.

As he started for home, he saw that the sun was setting and the sky was growing dark. "I must hurry or I shall be late for supper," said Peter.

"Take the short-cut along the top of the dike," his friend said.

They waved good-bye.

Peter wheeled his bike to the road on top of the dike. It had rained for several days, and the water looked higher than usual.

Peter thought, "It's lucky that the dikes are high and strong. Without these dikes, the land would be flooded and everything would be washed away."

Suddenly he heard a soft, gurgling noise. He saw a small stream of water trickling through a hole in the dike below.

Peter got off his bike to see what was wrong.

He couldn't believe his eyes. There in the big strong dike was a leak!

Peter slid down to the bottom of the dike. He put his finger in the hole to keep the water from coming through.

He looked around for help, but he could not see anyone on the road. He shouted. Maybe someone in the nearby field would hear him, he thought.

Only his echo answered. Everyone had gone home.

Peter knew that if he let the water leak through the hole in the dike, the hole would get bigger and bigger. Then the sea would come gushing through. The fields and the houses and the windmills would all be flooded.

Peter looked around for something to plug up the leak so he could go to the village for help.

He put a stone in the hole, then a stick. But the stone and the stick were washed away by the water.

Peter had to stay there alone. He had to use all his strength to keep the water out.

From time to time he called for help. But no one heard him.

All night long Peter kept his finger in the dike.

His fingers grew cold and numb. He wanted to sleep,
but he couldn't give up.

At last, early in the morning, Peter heard a welcome sound. Someone was coming! It was the milk cart rumbling down the road.

Peter shouted for help. The milkman was surprised to hear someone near that road so early in the morning. He stopped and looked around.

"Help!!" Peter shouted. "Here I am, at the bottom of the dike. There's a leak in the dike. Help! Help!"

The man saw Peter and hurried down to him.
Peter showed him the leak and the little stream of water
coming through.
Peter asked the milkman to hurry to the village.

"Tell the people. Ask them to send some men to repair the dike right away!"

The milkman went as fast as he could. Peter had to stay with his finger in the dike.

At last the men from the
village came. They set to
work to repair the leak.

94

All the people thanked Peter. They carried him
on their shoulders, shouting, "Make way for the hero
of Holland! The brave boy who saved our land!"

But Peter did not think of himself as a hero. He had done what he thought was right. He was glad that he could do something for the country he loved so much.

99

Story by Beverley Allinson
Illustrations by Barbara Reid

Effie came from a long long line of ants.
She was an ant like hundreds of others—
in every way but one.

All the others had tiny ant voices.

Effie's voice was like thunder.

Whenever she spoke, the whole nest of ants ran to get away from the noise.

One day, Effie set out to find someone who
would listen to her. Before long a caterpillar
wriggled into sight.

"NICE DAY, ISN'T IT?" said Effie.

But she was talking to thin air.
The caterpillar almost split his skin in his hurry
to escape.

Next minute, a butterfly landed beside her.

"HELLO THERE!" Effie boomed.

But the butterfly was blown away
and Effie was alone again.
Disappointed, but still hopeful,
Effie climbed a grass stalk for a different view.

**"WHERE IS SOMEONE
TO TALK TO?"**
she wondered.

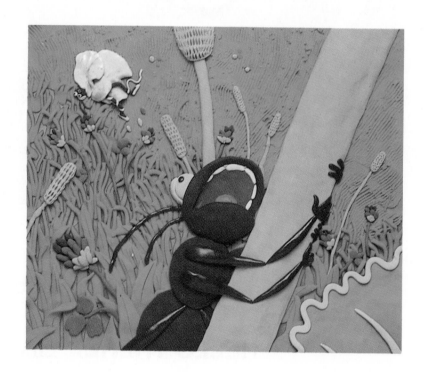

Her voice shook a web nearby, and a spider crawled out to see what she had caught.

"HOW DO YOU DO? WHO ARE YOU?"
Effie began.

But the web snapped.
Without a word, the spider
parachuted to safety and
was gone.

Effie went on for a long time
without meeting anyone at all.
By and by she stopped to rest.

To her surprise,
the rock she was lying on
suddenly sprouted legs.
"HELLO THERE!"
said Effie.
**"HAVE YOU TIME
FOR A CHAT?"**

But the beetle flipped in fright.
He spun in a dizzy circle,
snapped to his feet,
and scurried away.

When she met a grasshopper, all Effie said was, **"HI!"**
Even so, the grasshopper didn't stay.

"DOESN'T ANYONE WANT TO LISTEN TO ME?"

Effie yelled to the treetops.

Just then the grasshopper came leaping back.

**"YOU'VE CHANGED
YOUR MIND?"**
said Effie hopefully.
But the grasshopper shook his head
and zigzagged out of sight.

Then the beetle ran her way.

"WELCOME BACK!"
säid Effie with open arms.
But the beetle scurried silently past.

**"HAVE YOU COME
TO TALK TO ME?"**
Effie asked the spider, who was next.
"At a time like this?"
gasped the spider, spinning by.

And the butterfly passed in a flap.
The caterpillar wiggled right up to Effie.
"Run for your life!" he puffed.

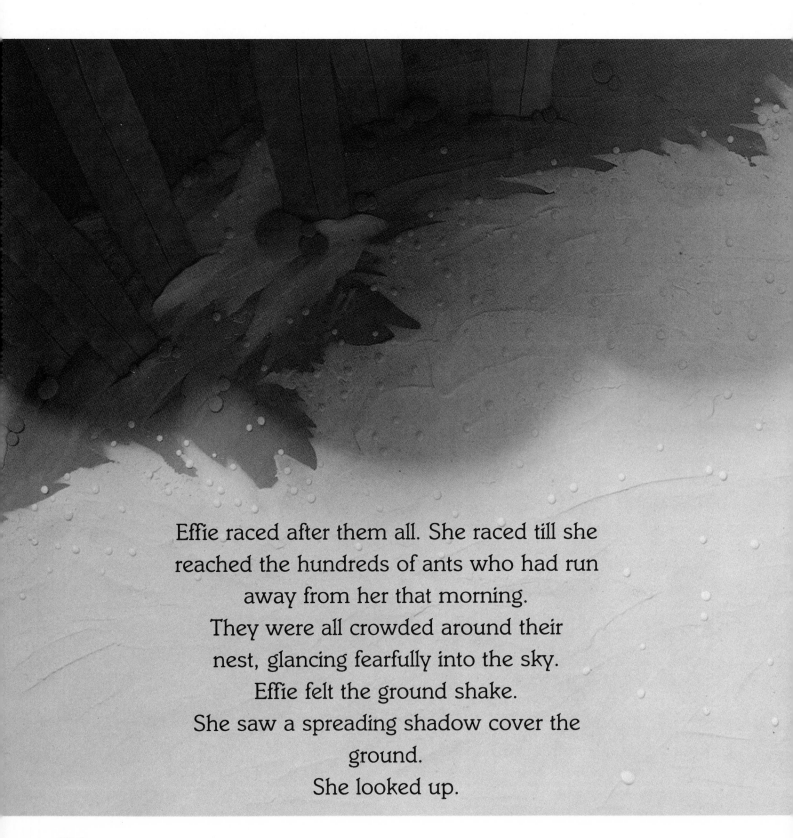

Effie raced after them all. She raced till she
reached the hundreds of ants who had run
away from her that morning.
They were all crowded around their
nest, glancing fearfully into the sky.
Effie felt the ground shake.
She saw a spreading shadow cover the
ground.
She looked up.

A huge foot was about to crush them all.

Effie took a deep breath.

"STOP!" she roared.
"HOLD IT RIGHT THERE."

"*Where?*" said an elephant,
looking around in surprise.

"**HERE!**" bellowed Effie.
"PLEASE WATCH WHERE YOU STEP."
"WATCH YOUR STEP!" echoed the other ants.

"*Oops,*" said the elephant,
suddenly noticing them all below.
"Sorry," she said and stepped nimbly aside.
Effie whooped and the ants cheered faintly
as the elephant's foot and
the near swish of her trunk missed them all.

"Who spoke up?" asked the elephant.

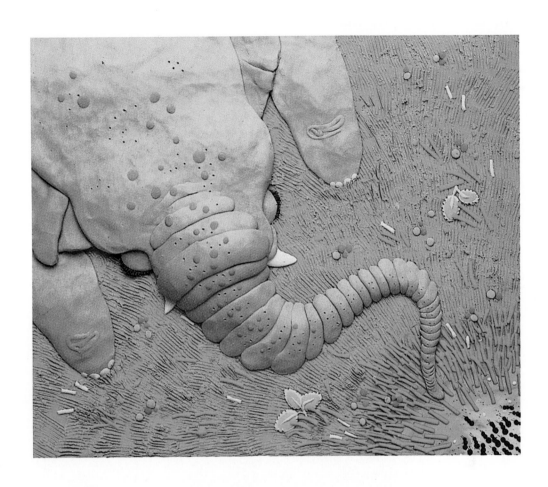

Effie waved an antenna to introduce herself,
and the elephant lowered her trunk to the
ground in greeting.

Effie climbed up, as if the trunk were a staircase,
until she and the elephant saw eye to eye.

**"I DON'T SUPPOSE YOU HAVE TIME
FOR A CHAT?"** she asked.

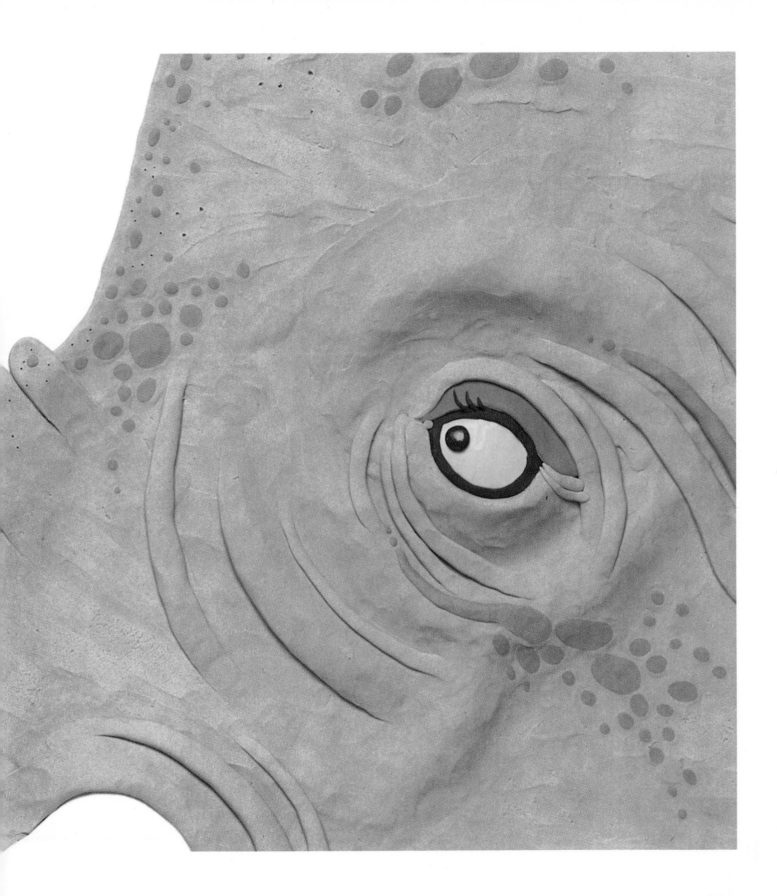

Effie and the elephant found
they liked each other enormously.
They talked for the rest of the day.

And for days and weeks and months after,
they met to talk of things large and small.

Before too long, large numbers of elephants
could be seen treading carefully through the
grass, watching their step
and chatting with their new friends.

LOREEN LEEDY

The Great Trash Bash

There are rolling hills and wiggly roads and shady trees in Beaston. It is a home to any animal that can run, fly or swim. But something is wrong.

The mayor is searching for an answer.

He talks to citizens wherever he goes.

At last, Mayor Hippo finds the answer.

To find out more about trash, the mayor goes
to the dump.

Next, he visits the incinerator.

The landfill is the last stop.

Mayor Hippo calls a town meeting.

At the meeting, the animals think of ways
to solve the trash problem. They start to
make changes in their everyday life.

Citizens take out their tools.

They start to clean up Beaston.

They even find some good uses for trash.

Soon, the town opens a recycling center.

In the recycling center, the trash is sorted out.

There are rolling hills and wiggly roads and shady trees in Beaston. It is a home to any animal that can run, fly or swim. Beaston is a beautiful place.

GLOSSARY

The **Glossary** can help you understand what words mean. It gives the meaning of a word as it is used in the story. It also has an example sentence to show how to use the word in a sentence.

The words in the **Glossary** are in ABC order. ABC order is also called **alphabetical order.** To find a word, you must remember the order of the letters of the alphabet.

Suppose you wanted to find *tram* in the **Glossary.** First, you find the **T** words. **T** comes near the end of the alphabet, so the **T** words must be near the end of the **Glossary.** Then, you use the guide words at the top of the page to help you find the entry word *tram.* It is on page 166.

A **synonym,** or word that has the same meaning, sometimes comes after an example sentence. It is shown as *syn.*

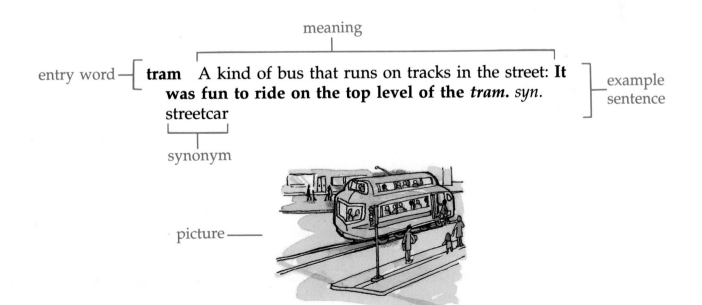

meaning

entry word — **tram**   A kind of bus that runs on tracks in the street: **It was fun to ride on the top level of the** *tram. syn.* streetcar

example sentence

synonym

picture —

bank

ad·mired   Looked at and liked something that seemed nice or beautiful: **All the parents at the open house** *admired* **the children's art work.**

bank   The land at the edge of a river: **Plants grew on the muddy** *bank* **along the side of the river.**

chat

chat   A friendly talk with someone: **Randy and Mario had a long** *chat* **and talked about what they did that summer.**

cit·i·zens   People who live in a town: **All the** *citizens* **of Newton wanted to build a new school.**

cot·tage   A small house: **The** *cottage* **made of red bricks had only four rooms.**

coun·cil   Meeting where people talk about something important: **The people held a** *council* **to talk about making some new laws.**

cottage

dan·ger·ous   Able to hurt someone or something: **Playing with matches is** *dangerous* **because someone can get burned.** *syn.* harmful

del·i·cate   Having a fine, tiny shape: **The small marks on the deer's back looked like** *delicate* **teardrops.**

dis·ap·point·ed   Feeling bad because hopes or wishes haven't come true: **Nick felt** *disappointed* **because he couldn't go to the zoo.**

dump   A large place where garbage is thrown away: **The city** *dump* **was filled with broken glass and old tin cans.**

dump

E

ech·o   A sound that is bounced back and heard again: **Jack shouted, "Hello" in the tunnel and heard the** *echo,* **"hello, hello, hello."**

eld·est   Oldest: **Aldo is the** *eldest* **child because he was born before his two sisters.**

en·er·gy   Power used to run machines: **The** *energy* **from a steam engine can make a train move quickly.**

e·nor·mous·ly   Very much: **Mrs. Chin danced, sang, and enjoyed herself** *enormously* **at our party.**

eldest

F

fan·cy   Looking very special: **The** *fancy* **box of crackers was covered with pictures of flowers.**

fool·ish   Not wise: **Leaving my raincoat at home during the storm was a** *foolish* **thing to do.** *syn.* silly

greeting

G

gloss·y   Very shiny and smooth: **Martha shined her shoes until they were** *glossy.*

greet·ing   Something you do that welcomes someone or says "hello": **Shaking hands or hugging is a friendly** *greeting.*

163

har·bor An area of water near shore where boats are kept: **The boats stayed in the *harbor* until the storm stopped.**

jetty

jet·ty A wall made of stone built in the water to stop the force of waves: **Powerful waves crashed against the *jetty* but did not reach the shore.**

lit·ter·ing Throwing trash and garbage on the ground and making a mess: **We must remember to stop *littering* in the park.**

littering

numb Not able to feel: **Nancy couldn't feel her toes because they were *numb* from the cold.**

pol·lut·ed Dirty and harmful to use: **The air was *polluted* by the thick, dark smoke.**

prop·er·ly The way something should be done: **Alma was able to walk *properly* again after her broken leg got better.**

quite   Completely: **Sam had not** *quite* **finished his book when he fell asleep.**

speckles

re•cy•cle   To make old cans, glass, or paper into new things: **Many families** *recycle* **empty bottles that can be made into new glass.**

S

scat•tered   Thrown around in different places: **A strong wind** *scattered* **leaves all around the yard.**

scur•ried   Ran quickly: **The squirrel was fast and** *scurried* **away from the dog.**

sight   Being able to see something: **Ana couldn't see the rabbits because they jumped out of** *sight.*

sobs   The sounds people make when they cry: **Megan tried to stop her little brother's** *sobs* **by wiping his tears and hugging him.**

speck•les   Tiny spots: **The** *speckles* **on the bird's eggs look like small dots.**

strapped

strapped   Held tight or tied with narrow strips: **Victor's book bag was** *strapped* **to his back.**

strength   Force or power to do something: **Clarence used all his** *strength* **to lift the heavy box.**

tearing

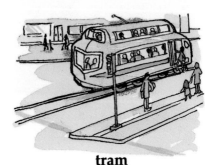

tram

trickling

wharf

tear·ing Ripping apart: **Joe was** *tearing* **up his old paper because he had made a new copy.**

temp·er The feeling of being angry: **The cat had a bad** *temper* **and hissed when someone tried to pet it.**

thun·der A loud sound that comes from the sky during a storm: **The booming noise after the lightning was loud** *thunder.*

tram A kind of bus that runs on tracks in the street: **It was fun to ride on the top level of the** *tram. syn.* streetcar

trick·ling Falling or moving very slowly or drop by drop: **The water** *trickling* **from the leak in the roof dripped into the pail.**

view What can be seen or looked at: **Andrea liked the** *view* **from the window because she could see the beach.**

wharf A dock or building near the water that is used for loading ships: **The men stood on the** *wharf* **and helped load boxes onto the boat.**